Relationship
RULES

12 Strategies for
Creating a Love that Lasts

JANICE HOFFMAN

PUBLISHING

PUBLISHING

www.RelationshipRules.com

Books may be purchased for sales promotion
by contacting the publisher:
Venus Publishing
P.O. Box 3694
Boulder, Colorado 80307
303-604-2222

Cover design: Barbara Greene
Copy edited: Chris Jacques
Author Photographer: Grant Oakes

Library of Congress Cataloging-in-Publication Data

ISBN: 978-0-9765588-0-4

1. Relationships   2. Self-Help   3. Psychology   4. Marriage

First Edition

Printed in Canada

Praises

Sarah Herold,
Director of Corporate Communications

"Unlike a lot of the advice books out there today, *Relationship Rules* is a wonderful reminder that love isn't about winning a competition or outsmarting someone else. When couples follow the rules, they will be enhanced by a lasting, healthy, loving relationship.

We all know that men and women are different. *Relationship Rules* has wonderful insights into leveraging those differences as positives to build a loving, respectful, mutually supportive relationship. Janice's advice is simple, backed by a huge amount of insight. Relationships can be so complex, but keeping them healthy doesn't have to be. Janice provides a clear path with accessible, simple ways!"

Douglas Brady,
M.Ed, Marriage & Family Therapist

"*Relationship Rules* is a practical, easy-to-use guide for men and women to create connection and intimacy in their love relationships. As a marriage and family therapist and relationship coach, I use the tools outlined in this book with my clients all the time. They are effective and easily applied in day-to-day living. The secrets to sustaining long-term intimacy are revealed in this simple how-to manual."

Karen Jones,
Land Developer

"This is a quick-read book. In accessible, simple ways it reinforces the importance of being kind to each other instead of a knee-jerk hurtful response. Stop and read *Relationship Rules* and find simpler, more successful, and happier solutions."

I dedicate this book to
Chase, Jenna, and Alex.

CONTENTS

INTRODUCTION

INTRODUCTION

Steve walks in the door after work, appearing stressed out. It doesn't take long for Anna, his wife, to take an interest in her husband's mood. To show she cares, she begins asking questions about his day. It takes no more than three questions before Steve begins to pull away. Not noticing the change in his behavior, Anna continues to ask more questions. Out of the blue Steve barks, "What's with all the questions?" Anna replies, "Why are you getting upset with me? I am just trying to show you I care by asking about your day." At this point, their emotions prevail, and communication stops.

Does this sound familiar? Couples often misunderstand each other because one simply doesn't know what the other needs or wants. Men and women are different—we know that—but we don't always know how or why.

If only Anna realized Steve needs time alone to de-stress and the last thing he wants to talk about is what is bothering him. It does not occur to her that when she asks questions, usually after three, Steve begins to feel like her questioning is more like an inquisition.

If only Steve realized Anna was asking him questions out of love. In a woman's world, asking questions is a sign of caring. In fact, the more questions she asks, the more she cares. In her world, if she does not ask questions, her behavior will be interpreted as insensitive.

The truth is Anna wasn't trying to upset Steve. By showing she cared, she wanted to make him feel better.

Interestingly, the opposite is true when a woman is stressed. Shari comes home from work feeling anxious. She is greeted by her husband, Jack, who gives her a hug. She begins telling him about her day. To Jack, it seems Shari is always complaining about a coworker. It does not take long for Jack to get annoyed. He interrupts and says, "Let it go. It's not that big a deal. Just don't talk to her." Shari immediately gets upset. To her, Jack's comments mean he wasn't listening. She's thinking, *My girlfriends listen to me, which lets me know they care.* In her frustration, she shouts, "Can't you just listen? Do you always have to try to fix everything?"

Jack is offended and responds, "I was listening!" In his mind, listening was exactly what he was doing. He can even repeat everything she said. Shari replies, "Yes, you were listening but you weren't hearing what I was saying." What Shari really means is, "Can't you just listen to me without interrupting and giving advice? Will you give me some verbal cues while I'm talking, so I know you understand? When I am finished talking, will you give me a hug and tell me everything will be okay?" Shari can't express herself this clearly and fails to communicate what she means. Jack is offended and confused, thinking he was being helpful. He can't understand why Shari accuses him of not listening. Feeling unappreciated for what he did do, he retreats to his office and logs on to his computer. Shari, feeling cut out of Jack's world, decides to give him the silent treatment the rest of the evening in hopes he will understand this is a big deal to her. Defenses are up and communication has stopped.

If only Jack realized that Shari needed an empathetic ear, he would have gladly given her one. She wasn't just complaining. Talking about what bothers her is one of the ways Shari relieves stress. He just didn't know. Jack was trying to show he cares by offering a solution. He wasn't trying to upset her.

Why be mystified about men and women and what they do? Take an active interest in the opposite sex, and you will reap the rewards. Possessing the necessary skills to communicate successfully will keep couples together. In fact, it keeps the passion alive.

The 12 relationship rules that follow shed light on how men and women can communicate at their very best. Practice each rule, add your own personality and style, and most of all, have fun!

How to Use This Book

How to Use This Book

Relationship Rules is designed as a guidebook for navigating through the ups and downs inherent in a love relationship. It is a guidebook for growing together in love and passion and a practical set of rules for creating a love that lasts.

Relationship Rules is meant to be used whenever your relationship is not what *you* want it to be. As you read through the various couples' stories as objectively as you can, try to see yourself in each scenario, applying that rule to your situation.

Women, as you read "For Women," consider your own personality when applying the suggestions. Keep in mind that trying new behaviors may feel awkward and unfamiliar. What matters is that you try, not how effortlessly you can pull it off. It is the time and effort you put into your relationship that counts. Making an effort is what your partner will notice most.

Men, as you read "For Men," try these suggestions using your own style. If at first you feel silly or think it won't work, push through the discomfort. Keep in mind, men and women are different and we need to learn new approaches for interacting with the opposite sex. This book is a tool for understanding how a woman thinks, what she wants, and how she feels. *Relationship Rules* makes understanding women easier.

If you try one of the suggestions, and it doesn't work, try again. Remember the first time you asked someone out. Did it feel awkward? It's the same with changing old behaviors into new ones.

Think about where you keep your toothbrush. If you moved it from the drawer to the medicine cabinet, how many times would it take for you to stop looking for it in the drawer before you remember now you keep it in the medicine cabinet? Experts say it takes 200 repetitions to change from one behavior to another. With that in mind, be patient with yourself and be patient with your partner.

I truly believe what we all strive, desire and yearn for, is to love and be loved. We aren't taught these relationship skills as children or even as adults. It is our responsibility to seek them out and learn them. It is my hope your lives will be richer, more enjoyable, and less stressful because of these relationship rules. May you always grow in love, in truth, and with passion.

THE RULES

The Rules

Rule #1.

Help your partner succeed in making you happy. *Leave hints, notes, or wish lists. In this way, a woman can get what she wants without asking directly, and a man can feel successful in making his partner happy.*

Rule #2.

Listen without interrupting. *Refrain from giving unsolicited advice or suggestions. Practice putting yourself in your partner's shoes.*

Rule #3.

Help your partner relieve stress. *Women relieve stress when they can talk freely about their emotions and feel heard and understood. Men relieve stress by disassociating themselves from their thoughts and feelings.*

RULE #4.

Appreciate your partner for their efforts, big and small. *Men are motivated by being appreciated; women are motivated by acts of caring.*

RULE #5.

Know how men and women keep score in a relationship. *Women grant points for the positive things men do, say, and give. Men give women big points for being let off the hook and for being appreciated.*

RULE #6.

Every day, pledge to give your partner one loving act, one affectionate gesture, one kind word or compliment. *Never miss an opportunity to tell your partner how much you care.*

RULE #7.

Know when to take a time-out. *Make sure you schedule time to talk later. Women especially need to know they won't be forgotten or blown off.*

RULE #8.

Set aside time to spend together at least once a week. *This is your time to reconnect, not to discuss finances, children, or careers.*

RULE #9.

Be aware of how you spend your sexual energy. *How you behave around the opposite sex will have an effect on how you relate to your partner.*

RULE #10.

Take responsibility for your own happiness. *By doing this you will find more peace and joy in your life.*

RULE #11.

Actively practice forgiveness, both for your partner and for yourself. *We all make mistakes. Forgiveness is the foundation of a strong relationship.*

RULE #12.

When you love someone, tell them. *Never assume they already know.*

RULE NO. 1

Relationship Rule No. 1

Help your partner succeed in making you happy. *Leave hints, notes or wish lists. In this way, a woman can get what she wants without asking directly and a man can feel successful in making his partner happy.*

Never before have men and women's roles been so parallel. Women don't need to be protected the way they used to be nor do they need a provider as in days long past. Women can even conceive babies through the use of a sperm bank. Many men today feel they are being pushed out of their traditional role of protecting, providing, and procreating. A wise man needs to know what today's woman truly wants.

One thing women want is romance and lots of it. Men are not taught how to be romantic. They have learned little about romance from their parents, the

16

media, or from watching others. Women, on the other hand, are born with a romantic gene, so romance comes naturally and effortlessly. Knowing this, how can a man be successfully romantic with a woman?

Mark knows he doesn't understand women. He tries his best to read Jenny's many moods and would be grateful to have some help in this department. Jenny has a different agenda. She holds out hope that Mark knows her well enough to give her what she wants. Jenny claims it's not romantic if she has to ask for what she wants. As close as they are, she thinks he should know her well enough by now to know her likes and dislikes.

There is no doubt Mark loves Jenny, but for the life of him, he can't read her mind. He tries and fails, tries and fails again, and eventually gives up. It is better to give up than to keep failing, he decides. Yet giving up should not be an option.

How can Jenny get Mark to be more romantic and

do the things she likes? The answer is to help him be successful in making her happy.

It is *not* romantic to ask your partner to cut flowers from the garden and put them in a vase. However, putting a vase or garden shears on the kitchen table may be just the hint your partner needs to recognize an opportunity to make you happy. It is *not* romantic to ask your partner to say "I love you." It *is* romantic to write "I love you" on the bathroom mirror or in an e-mail. In this way, your partner sees your playful side and is inclined to reciprocate. Enlist your imagination. Being playful is crucial to having a passionate, loving relationship.

In the first year of my own relationship, I had a chance to put this rule into practice. It started when I wanted my partner to write me little love notes like he did in the beginning of our courtship. I loved receiving the notes and saved every one. Not having received a note in some time, and missing the feeling they gave me, I decided one morning to ask him if he would write me a little note. He said he would, smiled and gave me a hug and left for work. A week or so went by and I still hadn't received a note, so again I asked, "Will you write me a little note sometime? I sure would love it."

I waited a few weeks and still no note. I decided to change my approach and make it easier for him. I left a pen and note pad next to where he kept his car keys but didn't say a word. The next morning, after he left for work, I went to the spot, and sure enough, there was a sweet note saying he loved me. In that moment I could feel his love. I felt connected to him and it made my day, which is what I was looking for all along. As long as there was a pen and paper next to his keys, I could count on finding a sweet little note every morning. Knowing I was loved helped me be more accepting of the people around me and more patient and kind. Even now, when we argue or I feel down, I can bring out the box of notes and read through them to feel his love. Usually, that's enough to get me out of my mood and back to being the loving person I know I am.

Rule No. 1

FOR WOMEN:

Make a wish list of what you want. Start with small requests and go from there. Keep it next to your bed or some other place your partner can easily find it. This is especially handy around Mother's Day, anniversaries and birthdays. Providing a wish list gives your partner an opportunity to give you something without having to ask directly. It also gives him a chance to surprise you with something you really want. When a woman gets what she wants in a relationship, she feels more attracted to her partner and feels more passionate towards him.

FOR MEN:

It is in a woman's nature to give. Typically, women give what they think would make their partner happy. She wants you to be happy, so help her by telling her what you want. When you can communicate what is important to you and why, it helps her understand where you are coming from.

You are the only one who knows what you want. Provide her with a road map showing how to get there. Share with your partner how you want to be loved. Write your request on a note or in an e-mail. Make your own wish list of things you want. Keep it current and in a place that is known to you both.

A woman is motivated when she feels her efforts are acknowledged as having value. Don't forget to tell her when she gets it right. In addition, you score points when you tell her she has made you happy.

RULE NO. 2

Relationship Rule No. 2

Listen without interrupting. *Refrain from giving unsolicited advice or suggestions. Practice putting yourself in your partner's shoes.*

Communication is the number one reason relationships succeed and, sadly, the number one reason relationships fail. Couples talk to each other, but how much do they actually listen?

You can usually sense when your partner isn't listening to you. Likewise, your partner knows when you aren't listening. When two people aren't listening to each other, they are not communicating. Over a period of time, that lack of communication can breed resentment and eventually may destroy the love. Poor communication can show up as indifference, detachment, anger, or even aggressive behavior.

To communicate successfully, listen to your partner

when he or she speaks. Resist the temptation to interrupt. Resist planning what you want to say next while pretending to listen.

Imagine being upset with your partner for something they did. Before you know it, you're being told what you did wrong. Typically, your first reaction is to fight back and defend your position. Resist the urge and decide to listen fully to your partner without judging anything they say. Try it for five minutes. Listen with the sole intent of understanding how he or she feels. Don't try to determine who's right and who's wrong; simply let your goal be to understand how your partner is feeling. You might learn something surprising about yourself.

Lilly and Andy are at a friend's house for a party. They're having fun and everything is going well. At one point during the evening, Lilly tells a group of friends a story about her and Andy's recent trip to Hawaii. Andy, believing he's being helpful, jumps into the middle of her story and corrects her. Lilly starts to steam inside. Not only did he interrupt her, but he corrected her in front of their friends. She doesn't say anything to him at the time, but later when they're home, Lilly lets Andy know how she's feeling.

Their evening was ruined because Lilly was upset with Andy. Had Andy refrained from interrupting and correcting her in front of others, their evening would have ended more happily.

Interrupting can go both ways. Greg, an outgoing man and the owner of a new Harley motorcycle, is showing off his new pride and joy to his buddies. Michele, his wife, comes out with beers for the guys and overhears Greg tell the story of how he had the bike going 80 mph on Highway 1 along the ocean. Michele interrupts with a scolding comment about how next time he'd better slow down and be more careful. Greg feels like Michele is treading on his pride, and doesn't like being embarrassed and scolded in front of his friends. He doesn't say anything until later that evening when Michele tries to initiate intimacy. He isn't receptive; instead he feels the need to punish her for her behavior by being unresponsive.

Successful communication occurs when both parties feel they are heard. Interrupting prevents this from happening. When we listen, we have an opportunity to learn about our partner. When we interrupt, nobody is heard. By taking the time to listen to our partner, we learn more about them and create the opportunity to build trust, consideration, and respect.

An added advantage is that taking the time to listen can nurture our own self-esteem, building trust within ourselves.

FOR WOMEN:

For passion to grow in a relationship, listen fully to your partner. Listening is an art and a learned behavior. It doesn't happen automatically. To learn this behavior, first be aware of when you interrupt your partner. Self-awareness gives you a starting point for improving your listening skills.

When your partner talks to you, give him your full attention. Make eye contact with him. Listen intently. Resist the urge to give helpful suggestions. If you must give advice, save it for later. Often you'll find that after he's finished talking, you won't feel quite the need to offer your suggestions.

When your partner feels safe enough to share his feelings and you listen without interrupting or offering suggestions, you build trust. This trust is vital for him to continue to open up and share. Without this trust, a man will not share what is on his mind.

FOR MEN:

Listen to your partner when she talks. Even though it can seem like she has no point to her story, let her get it out. Hold back that automatic urge to offer a solution. In fact, if you can refrain from giving advice, you will be a hero in her eyes.

You are definitely *not* wasting your time while she talks. I reiterate, *you are not wasting your time when you listen to her talk.* You are doing two things. First, you are helping her reduce her stress by giving her your full attention. Second, you are filling her emotional need as a woman to be understood.

Take this a step further by acknowledging her feelings. Refer to a time in your life when something similar happened to you. If you can't recall a time, think of someone you know who may have felt the same. When you empathize with her feelings, you not only help her relax and fill an emotional need, you also score points.

RULE NO. 3

RELATIONSHIP RULE No. 3

Help your partner relieve stress. *Women relieve stress when they can talk freely about their emotions and feel heard and understood. Men relieve stress by disassociating themselves from their thoughts and feelings.*

Men and women can get stressed out for different reasons. Consequently, they need to process and relieve their stress differently.

Women let go of stress by talking about what's bothering them. Men usually think, *Why on earth would you want to talk about what's bothering you and relive it all over again?* A man's perspective is to just forget about it, but a woman can't just forget. A woman needs to talk and does not understand her partner's attitude.

While men disassociate from negative feelings, women, due to the way their brains are wired, have a harder time disassociating. Not understanding this, a man wonders why his partner keeps dwelling on her problems.

When a man is stressed, he chooses to be left alone. He typically does not want to talk about what is bothering him. It's not until he has exhausted all possibilities that he will seek advice. In the meantime, he is reluctant to welcome any advice that is offered.

Here's an example of how a couple commonly deals with stress. Bob works for a large company on the verge of a significant round of layoffs. He's concerned for his job and how he will support his family. His wife, Maria, is also worried because his job is their main source of income. Trying to be helpful, Maria searches the Internet and prints a list of places where he can apply for a job should he get a pink slip. She approaches Bob, gives him the list, and wants to discuss his options. Bob has been thinking about his situation since he first heard about the impending layoffs.

Although he hasn't talked about it with Maria, he has been putting together his own game plan for what to do should he be laid off. He has his own way of processing the stress of his situation and wants to handle it alone.

They both have an agenda should Bob get laid off. They share the same goal, yet clearly have different approaches. Neither is right or wrong, just different. Bob prefers to process his stress alone. In Maria's world, it is a group effort.

Men have a keen ability to disassociate from their feelings. Women either express or suppress theirs. Disassociating from emotions does not come naturally or easily for a woman.

Women talk about their problems as a means of relieving stress. When women talk about their problems, it's as if the words must physically pass through their lips to relieve their stress. The process of talking about what's bothering them in the company of someone they trust is what allows them to relax. Knowing they are not alone and that someone understands them is crucial. When they know that their partner understands how they feel, they are then able to let go and move on. Without this kind of support from her partner, a woman may turn to a friend who *will* listen and understand.

An added benefit—when a woman talks about what is bothering her, many times she will discover the answer to her problem by talking with an empathetic listener.

FOR WOMEN:

Give your partner space, especially when he appears stressed. Men don't need to talk about their problems to relieve stress. They typically solve their problems alone or by disassociating from them for a time. It might look as if they are carefree and aren't concerned with a problem because they are playing video games, working in the garage or watching a sport, but it's time needed for letting go of stress. Don't deny your partner this time. Take comfort in knowing he appreciates your willingness to let him do his thing. Even if he doesn't say anything to you, he does notice your understanding. This support adds to the foundation of your relationship.

When you need to talk, try to remember how difficult it is for him to listen without offering advice. It is as difficult for a man to listen empathetically as it is for a woman to leave her partner be. Knowing a man's desire for love is greater than his need to pull away, patiently wait until he is ready to talk again.

FOR MEN:

When you are stressed, calmly let your partner know you need some time by yourself, and reassure her you'll come back. Reassuring her will help in letting you go. It will be easier for her to give you the time you are asking for when she knows you will be back.

Keep in mind women relieve stress by talking about what is bothering them. It is not the act of reliving a painful experience. Rather, it is sharing the experience with someone who cares and understands that relieves her stress. She may have no point, she may skip subjects, and it may even seem like she is complaining, but know she is not trying to make you miserable. She is expressing her feelings.

Give your partner clues that you are listening to her by nodding and maintaining eye contact. Offer reassuring comments to let her know you understand. Practice putting yourself into her shoes by recalling a similar situation and how it made you feel. She will be able to feel your sincerity, and you will both reap the benefits.

She will remember that you listened without trying to fix her. It is a big return on your investment when she reflects back on those times and thinks lovingly of you.

Rule No. 4

Relationship Rule No. 4

Appreciate your partner for their efforts, big and small. *Men are motivated by being appreciated; women are motivated by acts of caring.*

How many times have you felt your efforts to reach out weren't recognized and appreciated? Have you felt like whatever you do isn't enough or worse yet—isn't good enough? Perhaps this has occurred more times than you care to remember.

Your "reservoir of love" needs to be filled for you to feel loved. When primary emotional needs are fulfilled, you're motivated to express your feelings and have understanding for your partner. However, men and women have different emotional needs and different reservoirs.

A man needs to know his partner appreciates his efforts because appreciation fills his love reservoir, boosts his self-esteem, and motivates him to do more for her. Because of this desire for appreciation, a man naturally gravitates toward places where it is expressed. If he's appreciated at work, he spends more time at the office. If he finds it with his friends, he's drawn to spend time with them. If he's appreciated when playing sports, he indulges himself there.

A woman craves appreciation as well, but more importantly, she wants to know her partner cares. She likes to be cherished, to be desired, to be treated special. This is something men don't know instinctively. A woman can teach her partner how to make her feel special. It can be as simple as telling him what is important to her.

A man appreciates knowing which direction to take rather than going through a variety of actions hoping one of them will make his partner happy. If both partners clearly understand what is desired, both will benefit, and the relationship will deepen.

FOR WOMEN:

Let your partner know you appreciate his efforts to connect with you. When he demonstrates he cares, acknowledge this by giving him a response. Appreciate him for coming home every night from work. Acknowledge him for his contribution to housekeeping and child care. Even if you don't like the way he does a household task, find *something* he did that you appreciate and thank him for that, no matter how small. Don't wait until he does something major to show your appreciation.

Rule No. 4

FOR MEN:

Find ways to let her know you care with actions that say "I love you." Do the unexpected: a soft gentle non-sexual touch in passing, a note saying you love her, a helping hand with chores, a meal prepared especially for her, an endearing message sent by e-mail, even a glass of wine brought to her unexpectedly. Mix in different random acts of kindness to delight and surprise her. A good rule of thumb: a woman measures your love for her by your behavior.

RULE NO. 5

Relationship Rule No. 5

Know how men and women keep score in relationships. *Women grant points for the positive things men do, say, and give. Men give women big points for being let off the hook and for being appreciated.*

Women need to know their partner cares about them and that they are loved. When a woman knows her partner cares, she becomes confident in his love and can relax. Life is easier. Knowing she is loved, she can lean on her partner. When problems arise, she is better able to let them go because she knows he will be supportive.

If a woman is upset with her partner for making a mistake, she tends to ask him why he did what he did. Whatever his answer, it won't be the right one because she wants his mistake to go away. This is the one thing he can't deliver. At this point, an argument may follow. Over time, this arguing can wear down the terrain of a relationship and leave the relationship flat and passionless.

Have you ever pulled into your garage and realized you had forgotten to pick up something on the way home? Did you walk in the door and announce to your partner that you forgot? Probably not. We don't normally announce our mistakes. It isn't healthy for our self-esteem, and it probably would not do much for our relationship.

In a man's world, his unwillingness to communicate might stem from his fear that if he does communicate his mistakes and feelings, he might hear about them in future conversations.

Women benefit whenever they are able to let their partner off the hook. When you decide it isn't worth arguing about you send a message to your partner that getting along is more important than being right. Men appreciate it when their partner overlooks their mistakes, even if they don't say so.

We're all human and we all make mistakes. Let those negative feelings go whenever possible.

FOR WOMEN:

Men prefer women to be direct and short in their requests, so communicate as directly as possible and ask for what you want. If you aren't asking your partner for anything, he'll assume he is giving enough. So ask for what you want, be patient, and let him progress at his own speed. Men don't need a lot of information, just specific requests. You may have to ask more than once. Each time, ask as if it is the first time, without reminding him you asked before.

As best you can, let go of the idea, *If he loves me, he'll know what I want.* The truth is he doesn't *always* know what you want. It doesn't mean he doesn't care; it just means he doesn't know. He'd like to know and just needs your help.

FOR MEN:

Remember to set a happy tone, do the little things. That's what counts. Find out what she likes but won't do for herself. Listen for hints when she's talking. Keep an ongoing list. Light a candle, put on soft music, or draw her a bath. Slow dance in the kitchen. Give her presents that show you care. In her mind, the fact that you went out of your way for her is in direct proportion to how much you care.

Don't stop there. Women need to hear words of love as well as see actions that demonstrate you care. Tell her you love her, compliment her, leave her a note or write her a letter.

The reward for your hard work is a loving, more trusting partner. When a woman feels loved, she is better able to focus on what you're doing right in your relationship versus what you're doing wrong. When she's happy, you're happy, and all is well. A happy woman wants to appreciate her partner and his efforts. She will want to give back because she wants you to be happy, too.

RULE NO. 6

Relationship Rule No. 6

Every day, pledge to give your partner one loving act, one affectionate gesture, one kind word or compliment. *Never miss an opportunity to let your partner know you care.*

Make it your personal goal every day to let your partner know you love them through loving gestures. Actively show you care by saying "Thank you" or "I appreciate you for ____." Even if it feels like your partner hasn't done anything worth appreciating, thank them for being a part of your life, for their ongoing support, friendship, and love.

A good way to get in touch with this rule is by making a list of at least ten things you appreciate about your partner. Keep this list handy and use it. Share with your partner the different ways you are thankful for them in your life.

Communicate your love by sharing a sincere hug before going to work, instead of a quick hug. Find your partner when you first arrive home and say hello. Gently touch them when you pass in the hall to show affection.

It is not the magnitude of the gesture that counts; it is the love behind it. Taking time every day to express your love is a secret for creating passion.

Who doesn't want to hear the words "I love you" from their partner? Women generally have a greater need to hear these words. Say them whenever you feel love for your partner. Don't hesitate and don't let your ego interfere. If your heart feels the love, express it fully.

When your partner tries to express their love, don't blow them off because you're busy. Don't shrug off a hug when they offer one. When they give you a compliment, don't discount it for any reason. Instead, make eye contact with your partner and say "Thank you." Savor their loving kindness. Acknowledge your partner and tell them how good they made you feel. Accept the love. Acknowledge that you are worthy of receiving their love. You deserve it.

FOR WOMEN:

Demonstrate your love rather than verbalizing it. For a man, the act of love is more important than hearing the words.

Ask your partner what makes him feel loved or special. Maybe it's an e-mail from you, maybe it's preparing his favorite meal, or perhaps it's inviting him upstairs.

You can also show your love by not pointing out his mistakes. When a man is let off the hook, he feels appreciated.

FOR MEN:

Women need to know they are attractive to their partner. Feeling attractive creates attraction. Compliment her on how she looks. Use words other than *fine* or *nice*. Being told she's *sexy* or *beautiful* is music to her ears.

It is just as important to acknowledge her accomplishments. If she's a stay-at-home mom, tell her you notice how loving she is towards the children. If she works outside the home, tell her you appreciate how hard she works.

Women take "who they are" very seriously. Not surprisingly, women thrive in a relationship with someone who appreciates their efforts. Practice this by reminding her often she is both loved and lovable.

A smart man is one who creates different ways to show his love to his partner and demonstrates it often. By doing this, he can relax, knowing his partner feels loved.

RULE NO. 7

RELATIONSHIP RULE No. 7

Know when to take a time-out. *Make sure you schedule time to talk later. Women especially need to know they won't be forgotten or blown off.*

Arguments in a relationship are normal. How one argues can be critical to the survival of a relationship. Like so many other behaviors, men and women argue differently.

Men argue with one goal in mind—to get their partner to agree with their point of view. If met with resistance, they may become angry and/or aggressive. Given this agenda, in a heated conversation if a man's partner disagrees with him, the conversation can go south in a hurry.

On the other hand, when a woman argues with a man, she has multiple goals in mind. First, she wants to get her point across. Second, she wants to understand her partner's point of view. Lastly, she wants to resolve the argument. All three goals play a part in her behavior.

A woman's brain is wired differently than a man's. This enables her thoughts to travel at lightning speeds between both sides of her brain. The result is the side that feels anger and the side that feels compassion seemingly operate at the same time.

As men know, women have the ability to remember unkind words spoken in anger for many years. Unfortunately, when women get upset in the present, they recall those unkind words said in the past and let their partner know they haven't forgotten. This is one of the worst things women can do. Using this technique is one of the main reasons men shut down and will not communicate their feelings.

It is inevitable that men and women will have arguments. What's a couple to do? First, notice if your communication is deteriorating. Has one of you become defensive? It takes only one of you to develop this awareness and change the climate of the conversation. Second, take charge and stop the argument by taking a stand and saying, "This conversation is going nowhere. Let's take a time-out and talk about this later when we have had a chance to calm down and cool off. Can we talk again tonight after the kids go to bed?" The translation is, "I love you so much that I don't want to argue with you. I don't want either of us to say things we may regret. I want us to avoid being hurtful to each other. Let's talk about this later when we can come from that loving place we share, rather than from a position of righteousness."

In the heat of an argument, of course, couples aren't able to speak so lovingly. Each is too focused on their own point of view. That's exactly why it is so important to have the presence of mind to ask for a time-out. This act is a clear sign of your love and commitment.

FOR WOMEN:

For the sake of your relationship, swallow your pride and call a time-out before the conversation deteriorates completely. The sooner you can get your partner to agree to a time-out, the better.

Understand that when you or your partner becomes defensive, true communication breaks down. When you notice his defenses are up, it's in your best interest to ask for a time-out.

You may have to ask twice. He can't listen to you *and* understand you at the same time. Most people don't hear half of what is said to them when they are angry, so be prepared to ask him for a time-out more than once.

FOR MEN:

Tame your anger by remembering that your responsibility is to preserve the relationship. Expressing your anger will only put more distance between you and the person you love. The more you argue, the more difficult it will be to become close again.

After a woman speaks her mind, she then feels her emotions. She will go over the argument in her head or with a friend, analyzing it to a point that would exhaust any man. Finally, she will come to her own conclusion. Despite a whirlwind of emotions, she holds true to her perception.

Do yourself a favor and ask your partner for a time-out before things escalate. If you tell her you are afraid your words might become critical and/or cruel, you'll tend to have more success. Women, wishing to avoid this impending outcome, will hear the truth in your comment and back off. When asking for a time-out, you may have to ask more than once. Calmly stop the argument and take time to cool off.

Make sure you specify a time when you will come back and talk to her again. With this reassurance, she will willingly agree to take a time-out.

RULE NO. 8

Relationship Rule No. 8

Set aside time to spend together at least once a week. *This is your time to reconnect, not to discuss finances, children, or careers.*

This rule is the secret to keeping the passion alive. Often times after couples get married and have children, they stop taking time for themselves as a couple. Date night goes away. Romance fades. Routine sets in.

In today's world, couples are busy, finances are tight, and hiring a baby-sitter is easier said than done. They don't realize that not taking time for date night will have a negative impact, especially over a period of time. For relationships to grow, couples need to spend quality time together. If they put their relationship foremost in their lives, they will reap the benefits for years to come.

We put time and energy into our families, our careers and our finances. We recognize the importance of health by exercising and eating well. We attend classes on subjects that we enjoy. All of this is beneficial. Leading a balanced life is important, but if we want a life that includes passion and intimacy, paying attention to our relationship is paramount. We *must* put our relationship at the top of our list of priorities if we want our love and passion to grow. If we don't attend to our relationship, it will suffer.

Recent studies conducted in Denver, Colorado, reveal that couples separate because of unrealistic expectations. Believing a relationship will take care of itself may work for a while, but when it doesn't work, we risk losing our relationship. How empty our lives would be without that special someone.

If we don't nurture our relationship by spending quality time together as a couple, we can lose our desire for our partner. When we lack interest in our partner, we are less attracted to them and less involved in what is important to them. We neglect doing the things that show we care. Consequently, our affection wanes and so does the desire for intimacy and sex. When a relationship reaches this point, it resembles living with a roommate. A host of problems and temptations that are unhealthy for the relationship can arise.

Avoid this risk. Make spending time with your partner a priority. Together, get out your calendars and schedule a special date. Write in big letters or with red ink. Your date can be for a short period of time, even an hour or two will do. It doesn't have to be an expensive date. It is just the two of you spending time alone. Go to a park, take a hike or have a picnic. Don't let anything, barring emergencies, interfere with your scheduled time.

As the date draws near, let your mind wander. Let your imagination take over and fantasize about how you might spend this special time with your partner. Entertain only positive images. Think about where you might go, what you might do. Picture yourself having a great time. This is a very healthy and necessary mental exercise.

Make sure you don't use this time to talk about the kids, money, or careers. Use this quality time to your advantage and talk to your partner about your dreams and your goals. Reconnect. Plan future times together. As you do, you will learn things about your partner you might never have known. This is the secret to keeping the passion alive.

FOR WOMEN:

In years past, men were not required to spend quality time with their mates in order for their relationships to last. Women were content that men protected them, provided for them, and came home safely.

Today, a woman's survival is not dependent upon a man. Women want men to be something they have never had to be before: emotionally supportive. However, this support doesn't necessarily come naturally to a man. He needs to be coached. Date night is a perfect opportunity to build his emotional strength and teach him what you need.

You may not think you need a date night with your partner and easily dismiss this important relationship rule. However, it is critical that you make time to nurture your relationship. Spending time with your partner away from the checkbook, kids, and work will bring the two of you together. Harmony and a sense of well-being are benefits of living your life in balance.

Quality time with your partner will create trust. Men need to know their partner trusts them, and this is a great opportunity to develop trust in him.

You may have to be responsible for lining up a baby-sitter and picking the activity. It may not be perfect every time. That's okay. What is important is making time to spend together to reconnect with each other. Perhaps you can take turns getting the baby-sitter and making plans. In this way, you won't feel like the responsibility is always on your shoulders.

Tell him you appreciate him going on your date and you enjoyed spending time together.

FOR MEN:

For a woman to grow in love with her partner, she needs to feel he's on her side. You are her best friend and confidant, not just her lover. Making time for her gives a clear message you value her company.

She also needs to know you respect and understand her. Having date night provides a perfect opportunity to demonstrate your loving feelings. You can show your respect by opening a door, asking questions about her day and not looking at or talking about other women. Let her know you understand by listening to her talk about her feelings without interrupting or giving advice.

Make sure you take turns planning date night, so it doesn't feel like one person's responsibility. When you take charge and make date night arrangements, she will interpret this as a sign of caring. The further in advance you make plans, the more special she will feel. Avoid waiting until the last minute when it's your turn to plan the date.

Remember, this is a time to reconnect with your partner and recall all the reasons she's the one you love.

RULE NO. 9

Relationship Rule No. 9

Be aware of how you spend your sexual energy.
How you behave around the opposite sex will have an effect on how you relate to your partner.

Should you tell your partner you ran into an old boyfriend or girlfriend, surfed the Internet for beautiful bodies, or had lunch with someone of the opposite sex? Have you ever done something and wondered if you crossed the line of faithfulness? When do these actions affect your relationship? When are they considered cheating?

The answer: it becomes a problem in your relationship when your romantic, sexual energy is pulled away from your partner and is directed toward another person. Your relationship is negatively affected when you purposefully omit details about your whereabouts or how you spend your time.

In the seven years Bob and Laura have been married, they have been completely faithful to each other. Two months ago, Bob's father passed away and he has been grieving, as one would expect. One day, home alone and feeling down, he logged on to the computer to check his e-mail. As usual, he recognized junk mail from various porn sites. Normally he would delete the messages but grieving and coupled with the fact that he and Laura hadn't had sex in weeks, he clicked on a link that promised photos of gorgeous, naked women. He checked out the women, and a few minutes later closed the window and opened another to see how his stocks were performing.

Did Bob do anything wrong? There's nothing wrong with having a healthy curiosity. However, had Bob continued to cruise porn sites or visited chat rooms to e-mail women advertising on the site, he would be using his sexual energy in an unhealthy way, and he would be placing his relationship at risk. It is important for his relationship to reserve his sexual energy for Laura. In fact, spending his sexual energy outside the relationship could be very costly.

Debbie and Sam dated for two years before they got married. In the beginning of their relationship, they experienced a lot of passion. They could hardly keep their hands off one another. After the initial glow wore off, Debbie thought Sam's attraction for her was waning. She wasn't sure what to do and was worried Sam didn't care as much for her as he did when they were first dating.

One day on her way home from work, Debbie stopped at the store to pick up groceries. While standing in line to pay for the items, she is surprised to see that the person in front of her is her ex-boyfriend Kevin. Debbie says hello and after exchanging how are you's, Kevin asks, "So, are you married now?" This is her defining moment. If she says, "Yes, I am," she gives Kevin a clear message that her commitment is to her marriage. By giving that commitment a voice, she empowers herself and strengthens her bond with her partner, Sam.

In an effort to see what Kevin would say next, she could answer, "Yes, but this last year has been rough. I don't know how much longer we will be together." In this scenario, her answer also defines her level of commitment. Debbie's response minimizes her relationship with Sam by discounting her love for him. Even if she does not mention this to Sam, it will affect his trust in her. Telling Kevin she is happily married is clearly the choice that will demonstrate Debbie and Sam's love for one another.

We constantly make choices about our relationship. When you wake up each morning, the way you greet your partner, or *don't* greet your partner, is a choice. Do you say good morning before you get out of bed? Do you make a point of giving your partner a hug or kiss before leaving for work? How you spend your affection is a choice. We also have a choice about how we spend our sexual energy. When you reserve it for your partner, your sexual attraction grows. When you use your sexual energy to gratify the ego by flirting and beyond, your attraction for your partner lessens.

If you find yourself fantasizing about another person, think of your partner instead. Recall what you find attractive about him or her. Remember how excited you become when thinking about your partner. Imagine your partner in sensual ways. Train your mind to think about your partner when you find yourself fantasizing about another. In time, you will automatically think of your partner. Don't be surprised if using this process puts you in the mood to seek out your partner and do what comes naturally.

FOR WOMEN:

Men need sex; women need to talk. Just as communication is important to women, sex is important to men. This is simply how men and women are wired.

Use your sexual energy in a healthy way. Instead of flirting with another man to see if you are still attractive, use that sexual energy in a way that serves your relationship. Focus your sexual interest on your partner. If you find yourself thinking about another man, bring your awareness back to your partner and fantasize about him. Imagine sensual images of you and your lover. Try new creative ways to be intimate together and discover new heights of excitement. When you are in touch with your sexual energy and direct that energy towards your partner through images, touch, and action, you will experience more passion.

If you need ideas, Linda Korn has written several

books that give easy step-by-step instructions on how to create sensual nights of romance and sex. They include, *101 Nights of Great Sex,* (HarperCollins, 1999) and *101 Quickies,* (HarperCollins, 1997). These books will give you many ideas to spark your imagination.

Rule No. 9

FOR MEN:

It is normal and instinctive for a man to look or think about other women. You do not need to feel guilty about it; you just need to be aware of how you spend your sexual, romantic energy.

It is normal to find another woman attractive, but don't let your romantic energy drift away from you. If you do, it can show up in your partner in negative ways. Your partner may become jealous or insecure for seemingly no apparent reason. Should this happen, know at some level she will sense your wandering mind. As best you can, whenever your thoughts drift toward another woman, replace that image with sexy ones of your partner. Reel in your wandering mind and focus your attention on how sexy you find your partner.

Deep down, she is who you want to be with, so redirect your thinking. If you train your mind to do this, in time it will happen automatically. *See pretty woman. Think of partner. Want to have sex.* Rather caveman in nature, but it's true.

RULE NO. 10

Relationship Rule No. 10

Take responsibility for your own happiness. *By doing this you will find more peace and joy in your life.*

Back when we were single, we decided what would be fun and what would make us happy. Our happiness was our responsibility.

Once in a relationship, we have someone to share that responsibility with—our partner. We unconsciously decide not to be as responsible for creating our own happiness, and we go on a mini-vacation. Yet, this absolute truth remains: we are responsible for all our thoughts, choices and actions, including feeling happy and sad.

It's been said, "Do not look to one person for your happiness." Yet, somewhere in the whirlwind of a new romance, we get swept away and fall in love. Instead of doing things just to please ourself, it also becomes our pleasure to do things to make our partner happy. When they light up with a smile, we light up even brighter.

Every loving man's goal is to have a happy woman as his partner. He takes credit for her happiness because, by his calculations, if she's happy, he *must* be doing something right.

A woman is happy when her partner can support her emotionally by making an effort to listen and empathize with her feelings. When he does this, she is happy. When he is not able to because he's otherwise occupied, her lack of happiness should not be his responsibility.

Sarah thinks the world of Bill. Since the beginning of their relationship, Bill has been the perfect partner. He calls when he is going to be late. He remembers holidays and special occasions. In the two years they have been together, Bill has done his best to show his love for Sarah.

One day, Bill forgets that he made plans to have lunch with Sarah. He missed writing it down in his day-planner. Sarah arrives at the restaurant looking forward to her lunch date with Bill. After waiting a half-hour, she leaves, upset and confused as to why Bill didn't show.

In Sarah's mind, Bill is great and does all kinds of wonderful things to make her happy. It is out of character for Bill not to show up at the restaurant. Now feeling unimportant, Sarah is not happy. She was content until Bill didn't show. By her calculations, it must be Bill's fault that she is now upset. She blames him for disturbing her peace.

In this situation, it is as if Sarah has made an unspoken, unconscious agreement with Bill to relinquish to him a large percentage of her "responsibility to be happy." Sarah holds Bill responsible for her happiness—a responsibility that Sarah previously held for herself. We do not realize we have made this agreement until our partner shows up late or forgets an important date. Whatever the reason for the indiscretion, we feel hurt by their actions and we become unhappy. Therefore, we decide, it must be our partner's fault.

Blame is the poison that contaminates relationships and causes couples to retreat from each other. A man will inevitably shut down in the relationship if he feels a woman blames him for her unhappiness. Relationships don't have to take this road. It was unfortunate Bill forgot his lunch date with Sarah, but her happiness is her choice. She can choose her mood independently of Bill's behavior.

To have a healthy relationship, be clear about this: No one is responsible for making you happy *except you*. Responsibility for your own happiness is also up to you. Any deviation from this truth can result in suffering.

Blaming your partner for your unhappiness won't make the situation better; it will only put distance between you. From the other side, being repeatedly blamed for your partner's unhappiness will take its toll on your relationship. Taking responsibility for your own happiness will empower you and make your relationship stronger.

In another example, Henry and Jeanette decide to go out for dinner to relax and unwind after a long day at work. As he pays for the meal, Jeanette asks Henry how much money he spent during the week. Finances are a hot topic, and after three questions, Henry starts feeling like Jeanette is treating him like child, as if she doesn't trust him.

After arriving home, Jeanette heads toward the bedroom, slamming the door. She is obviously upset. Henry decides there's nothing he can do to make the situation better. He retreats to the family room, grabbing a beer and chips on the way. He turns on the TV, clicks through the channels, and instantly becomes one with an infomercial about vacation timeshares. It is the perfect distraction, and just what he needs to chill out and gain some objectivity about what had just happened.

After 15 minutes, Jeanette quietly comes out of the bedroom. She thought about what happened and realized how unkind she was. Jeanette wants to talk to Henry and make-up. She sees Henry watching TV, munching away on chips and drinking a beer. She leaves the room before Henry even knows she is there. She becomes even more upset. In her mind she's thinking, *How can he sit there relaxing when we just had a fight? I am anguishing over every word that was said and he doesn't care because he surely wouldn't be watching TV.*

Without fully understanding how men operate, Jeanette's reaction leads to more separation. She distances herself from Henry because she assumes that he doesn't care. She doesn't realize his behavior is not a true reflection of how much he cares. What Jeanette also doesn't realize is because of the way men are wired, they have the ability to disassociate from their feelings. Henry is taking responsibility for his feelings by giving himself a break. In this way, he is taking responsibility for his own happiness.

When we are happy with ourselves—when we are not waiting for someone else to do something to make us happy—we stop blaming. Then, when our partner does something that makes us happy, we can see it as a gift, not an expectation. We can see these gifts as a *dessert* and not as the *crumbs* we've been waiting for. It's a matter of choice and perception. When we do this, we consciously create an environment in which we truly feel happy.

FOR WOMEN:

Make your own happiness a priority. Don't wait for your partner to do or say things to make you happy. Create routines and habits that you enjoy. Make a list of things you like to do. Does taking a dance lesson give you pleasure? Maybe spending one-on-one time with your children, having lunch with a friend, or watching a favorite TV show brings you happiness. Try different activities to see what you like. The more things you try, the more you will discover what you enjoy and what you do not.

As you take responsibility for your own happiness, your partner will take notice. He will be motivated to spend time with you because *your* happiness becomes *his* happiness.

As you master this attitude, you will feel more empowered. In fact, every time you take responsibilty, you empower yourself to be a better person. By this approach, you will not view your partner as a means to your happiness; you will see him as a gift. He will be happier simply because you are happy yourself.

FOR MEN:

Let your partner know her happiness is important to you. Be supportive of the things she likes to do. It might not be your "thing" to go for a walk or join a book club, but encourage her to do what she likes. Reassure her that you do not see her activities as taking time away from you, and there will still be plenty of time to spend together. Give her the reassurance she's looking for. Women with children think they have to be available in case anyone needs them, so tell her it's okay to spend time with a friend or alone.

Because of society's image of what the perfect woman is supposed to look like, women are overly concerned with their looks. High on this list are weight, hair, and clothes. She believes her looks dictate how attractive she feels inside. Communicate that it is how attractive she feels, and not how attractive she looks, that matters. Help her understand this concept. She doesn't understand because she was not taught this growing up. In fact, quite the opposite. Tell her what you find attractive about her.

Taking responsibility for personal happiness comes easily for men, yet women struggle with this one. Helping your partner with this will pay big dividends for you in the long run.

RULE NO. 11

Relationship Rule No. 11

Actively practice forgiveness, both for your partner and for yourself. *We all make mistakes. Forgiveness is the foundation of a strong relationship.*

One of the most important skills needed for a relationship to thrive is the ability to forgive—the ability to forgive yourself and your partner. Forgiveness leads us back to the love we have always felt.

One of our primary goals must be to master the art of forgiveness. Forgiveness is what allows us to have peace of mind. When we have peace of mind, we are more understanding. When we are more understanding, forgiveness comes more easily.

When we know we will be forgiven, we naturally are more accepting and appreciative of our partner. We feel more comfortable in their presence and can relax in that comfort. Love for our partner grows because we feel safe and secure. Our love will stand the test of time because we can forgive.

By not forgiving our partner, we store the hurt inside and risk creating resentment. Those resentments accumulate over time and have the potential of causing destructive behavior.

We usually know when we have made a mistake. It is not our intention to hurt our partner, but sometimes we do. We want our partner to understand that we did not mean to hurt them and would like to be forgiven.

When we are effected by a partner's mistake, we can get angry. We blame our partner for our unhappiness. Blame pushes them further away and comes with a price. We might be right, but the cost weakens our relationship. When we can access that place inside ourselves of *wanting* to forgive, we will draw our partner closer to us.

The power of forgiveness is immeasurable. Books have been written, songs have been sung, and ministers have preached its power. Acceptance, trust, and appreciation grow when we are able to forgive or be forgiven. Many people grew up with great role models who taught forgiveness and its value. For those not so fortunate, it is up to them to be self-taught.

How do we forgive? We start by putting ourselves in our partner's shoes and asking, "How would I want to be treated if I made that same mistake? Wouldn't I want to be forgiven?"

Don't withhold forgiveness for the sake of being right. Being right is a lonely place where there is room for only one. Forgiveness has room for all of us. Of course, you can be upset with what someone said or did, but you can choose to access that forgiving part of yourself that knows they would not deliberately hurt you. Your partner made a mistake, just like we all do, every day. When you can accept this truth, *wanting* to forgive them will come naturally.

Forgiveness is a gift we give ourselves as well as our

partner. As human beings, we are destined to make mistakes. But we are also designed with the capacity to forgive, if we so choose. When we can objectively look at our own mistakes without judgment and condemnation, forgiveness comes more easily.

When we admit to ourselves that we were doing the best we could, we can set ourselves free. One way to actively forgive is by consciously saying, "I didn't know better, but now I do." The next time that situation presents itself, we will make a better choice. Forgiveness is necessary because we aren't perfect.

FOR WOMEN:

Women freely use the phrase "I'm sorry," many times a day. Saying it doesn't take away from their self-esteem. But this is not so for men. A man's self-esteem is closely tied to finding the solution, getting the job done, and being right. It can be difficult for a man to admit he is wrong, and even more difficult to say the words, "I'm sorry."

When your partner accepts responsibility for his actions and comes to you with an apology, accept it as best you can. Wait! That doesn't mean automatically forgive him whenever he says, "I'm sorry." Accepting his apology does not mean you let go of what he said or did, and instantly become happy. It does mean you have heard his apology and have acknowledged it.

A man will stop apologizing if he feels his apology is not accepted. A man figures, *Why bother? She won't accept my apology anyway.* Avoid this by saying, "Thank you for saying you are sorry. I am still upset and need some time to contemplate what has happened." Even if you are still upset, this lets your partner know you have heard his apology, and need some time to process accepting it.

As you practice this rule, notice your partner's reaction to this new way of accepting his apologies. Accepting an apology changes the tone between the two of you from a "tug-of-war" to that of a "coming together." You are on the right track whenever you can shift to a more positive way of communicating. Whenever you can access that tender part inside yourself that knows, *This is a good man who loves me and doesn't want to hurt me*, then forgiveness begins.

Forgiving yourself is a good practice, too. Practice forgiving yourself daily for the small things. Put the big things on the shelf for now. Try forgiving yourself for being five minutes late to pick up your children. Forgive yourself for canceling an appointment at the last minute. Women are good at holding themselves to a high standard. If you practice forgiveness for the little things, you will find that when something big comes along, you will be better equipped to handle it. You will be more grounded and less emotional.

It is also important for women to understand how men approach forgiveness. When a man's feelings are hurt, his first reaction is anger. When he shifts to his logical side and assesses the reality of the situation, he then moves closer to forgiveness. His logical side thinks, *It is unfortunate this happened, but let's resolve this argument. Let's move forward and enjoy each other's company.* For him, forgiveness begins with a fresh start.

FOR MEN:

We all have a masculine and a feminine side. Think of your life as a balance scale. One side is female and one side is male. Each day you strive to be in balance as you go about your life. When you are able to practice forgiveness, you access the feminine side, bringing that scale more into balance.

It's easy for a man to remain on his male side. You work all day, play or watch sports, solve problems and fix things. The male side becomes heavier. When you have a misunderstanding with your partner and choose to apologize, you nurture your feminine side.

Living a life in balance is what brings us peace of mind. When a woman hears the sincerity in your apology, it has a powerful, positive effect on her. Before she can forgive you, she needs to hear the words, "I'm sorry." She will then measure, by your actions, if you are sincere. When your partner is hurting, communicate to her that you identify with her pain. Then she can let go, relax, and become a loving partner once again.

When you are hurt because of something she did, first acknowledge your feelings. If you feel sad, acknowledge this to yourself. If you feel betrayed or unimportant, let yourself experience those feelings, but do not dwell on them. Acknowledge them.

Next, in a calm tone, tell your partner what you are feeling. Tell her you feel hurt, you feel sad, or whatever the emotion may be. Give her the opportunity to communicate that she is truly sorry.

Women think men are tough through and through. They don't realize how sensitive a man can be underneath his thick skin. Express in words that you have feelings, which can be hurt. You know, deep down, she doesn't want to hurt you.

Without knowing this, she may try different approaches in an effort to make you feel better. This will just frustrate you both, so help her by communicating what you want. If you want time alone, let her know you need time to rejuvenate your batteries. As soon as you can communicate this to your partner, her ability to let you go with a smile increases exponentially.

Forgiveness takes time. Be patient with yourself. Be patient with your partner. Both of you *will* reap the benefits. Forgiveness leads us back to love and will grow over time by trusting in each other's actions.

RULE NO. 12

Relationship Rule No. 12

When you love someone, tell them. *Never assume they already know.*

"I love you." Our hearts purr every time we hear these words. Our world is validated, our stress reduced, our joy increased. Inside our bodies, hormones are released. We feel secure. We feel truly loved whenever we hear these words.

Every time someone says "I love you," we are given a gift that costs nothing and provides everything. We can pay that gift forward by telling others we love them. Never assume they already know.

Sometimes in relationships, we wait for our partners to say "I love you" first. Life is too short to be waiting to hear these words. Say it first, and you may be surprised at your partner's response. Those three little words just might be what he or she needs to hear at the moment and can make their day.

A woman tends to be more responsive than a man when she hears "I love you," especially when he backs up his words with actions. He can say "I love you" often, but if his actions do not support his words, she will tend to distrust that he means it. He needs to back up his words, with actions that support those words, so she will grow to trust his love.

To show he cares, a man will do useful things: Wash her car, run errands or change a light bulb. But because his actions are practical in nature, she doesn't interpret them as caring for her. Rather, she sees that he's simply doing his share, which does not feel romantic in her world. His attempts to communicate his love fly right past her because she's looking for signs of romance.

A man prefers his partner show love through her

behavior and actions. He likes to hear the words "I love you," but doesn't need to hear them as often. For example, if she lets him off the hook when he makes a mistake, he interprets that as love. When she tells him how happy he makes her feel, he interprets that as "I love you."

FOR WOMEN:

Romance comes easily to a woman, yet it is a man's nature to be practical. You can't grow in a relationship if you don't *feel* loved. By the same token, you can't grow in a relationship if you aren't *giving* love. Show him how you want to be loved and then allow yourself to *feel* his love. Ask him to hold you and then relax into that support. Consciously breathe his love into your body. Know this man loves you.

FOR MEN:

When you want to do something for your partner to show you care, opt for romantic gestures and leave the practical ones for another time. Place love notes where she can find them later. Write "I love you" in an e-mail, on a mirror, in chocolate syrup—you get the idea. Find your own ingenious ways to say, "I love you." Remember, delivering these words eye-to-eye and face-to-face is hard to beat. When you feel love for your partner, don't miss the opportunity to tell her.

Summary

For all the men and women who have attended one of my programs, you inspired me to write this book. May your love last a lifetime.

ACKNOWLEDGMENTS

ACKNOWLEDGMENTS

Two and one half years after I initially called John Gray's *Mars Venus* offices to inquire about starting a *Mars Venus* support group, receiving a telephone call was the last thing I expected. The directors of the *Mars Venus Institute,* Bart and Maia Berens, asked me if I wanted to be one of the first people John Gray would train to facilitate his famous *Mars Venus Workshop.* It must have been destiny calling. God calling, as I like to say. Who would have thought John Gray's office had kept my name and phone number for so long? I knew there was something very special about that phone call. I was being given a window to find my true passion.

At that time, I was writing guided meditations for a wonderful group of people who gathered once a week for a homemade lunch and one of my meditations. I was also facilitating an *Attitudinal Healing* support group and *A Course In Miracles* group which met weekly. Teaching the *Mars Venus Workshop* seemed like a perfect fit in my world.

Two months after that call, I met John Gray and his staff of remarkable people. At my training, I listened with great interest to John speak about the many ways in which men and women are different. That week was a major turning point in my life, and by the last day, I clearly knew my purpose for being there.

I knew when I called two years prior, I wanted to be part of the *Mars Venus* world John Gray had created. Meeting his staff and training with other facilitators felt like I was at a homecoming with people I had known since childhood.

I poured my soul into being the first and most successful facilitator with the *Mars Venus Institute.* I was John Gray's "Star Facilitator." From there, I went on to help train, coach and mentor over 550 *Mars Venus* facilitators and counselors worldwide. My curiosity and passion for gender differences has continued to grow to this day.

I want to thank John Gray for being my teacher. John, because of your excitement, your compassion, your knowledge, and character, I have found my true passion, my love of life. Thank you for allowing me to be the messenger for your Mars Venus work which has touched so many lives. Thank you for being a wonderful role model and teacher. I am so grateful you are a part of my life. Our mutual passion, helping others learn about gender differences, is the inspiration for this book.

Another person responsible for my being able to write this book is my former husband, Charlie Hoffman. Your help has made it possible for me to write this book and I thank you for your constant support. Thank you for being flexible so I could take advantage of the opportunities presented to me. Thank you for teaching me to be clear in my communications. I have been able to pursue my passion, and words cannot express my gratitude. Thank you from the bottom of my heart.

Clearly, John Gray and Charlie Hoffman have been

very instrumental in my life. Because of these special men, I have been able to accomplish my lifelong dream of writing this book.

Thank you, Dan Maher, for your steady commitment and loving support in the publishing of this book. I knew I was never alone in this endeavor because of you. The many hours you spent on this book, coaching me and encouraging me, will never be forgotten, neither will the love behind them.

Thank you Dr. Judith Briles. I don't know what I would have done without your guidance and direction. You kept me focused and on the right path with the right people.

Ronnie Moore of WESType Publishing Services, Inc., thank you so much for your help in getting this manuscript to print. You are a lifesaver and I can't thank you enough.

I want to acknowledge this book's biggest supporter and friend, Dorie McCubbrey, M.S.Ed., Ph.D.

Dorie, your professional skills as the author of *How Much Does Your Soul Weigh?* (HarperCollins 2003) are exceptional. Your emotional support is invaluable. You have been there whenever I needed you. Your sense of humor has kept me going on days when going wasn't what I had in mind. Your own accomplishments as an author, professional speaker, and counselor have inspired me to be more of who I am. Thank you for your constant support and guidance.

Thank you, Barbara Greene, my graphic designer. Working with you is effortless because we share the same vision.

Thank you, Christine Jacques and Rebecca Finkel, for your expertise and guidance.

Thank you to my colleagues from the National Speakers Association and the Colorado Independent Publishers Association, who have offered their support and expertise along the way. Each one of you played a part in this book.

Thank you to my children, Chase, Jenna, and Alex. It is the love we share which motivates me to be the best mom I can. Throughout my career, your love and encouragement have inspired me so much. Thank you for being you.

A special thanks to my daughter, Jenna. I appreciate your expertise and knowledge, but most of all, your honesty. I will never forget the laughs we had working together on this book.

I want to also acknowledge my family and circle of friends. Because of your constant love and support, I had the courage to write and publish this book. I am so very grateful to all of you for being a part of my life.

Order your copy today!

Please send me _____ autographed copies of *Relationship Rules* by Janice Hoffman for $16.95 plus $3.00 for shipping. Additional copies: add $1.00 each for shipping.

Name _____

Address _____

City/State/Zip _____

Phone _____

Email _____

Autograph Request _____

Please charge my:
☐ Visa   ☐ MasterCard   ☐ American Express
☐ Personal check   ☐ Cash

Card No. _ _ _ _   _ _ _ _   _ _ _ _   _ _ _ _

Exp. Date _ _ / _ _

Janice Hoffman, *Relationship Expert*
P.O. Box 3694 • Boulder, CO 80307
Phone: 303-604-2222
www.RelationshipRules.com
Email: Info@RelationshipRules.com